THE
Old Photographs
SERIES

THE COUNTY BOROUGH OF
MERTHYR TYDFIL

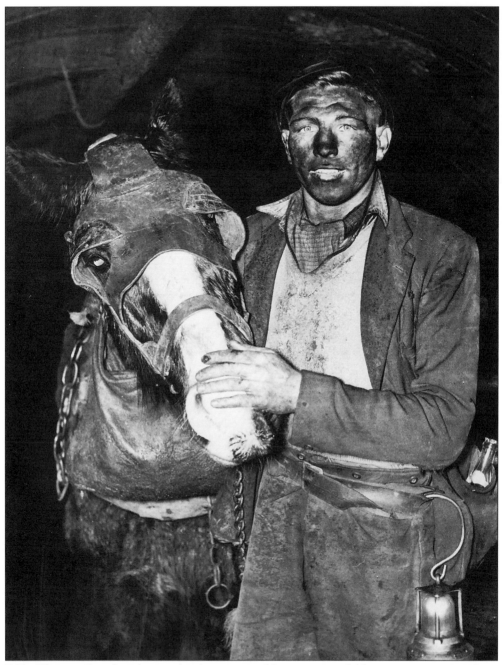

Eddie Thomas, British welterweight champion and later a successful boxing manager seen here at work c.1946 in the family level, Heolgerrig, Merthyr.

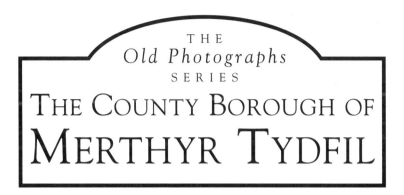

THE
Old Photographs
SERIES

THE COUNTY BOROUGH OF
MERTHYR TYDFIL

Selected by
Carolyn Jacob, Stephen Done and Simon Eckley
From the collections of
Cyfarthfa Castle Museum and Merthyr Tydfil Public Libraries

**ALAN
SUTTON**
BATH • AUGUSTA • RENNES

First published 1994
Copyright © captions Carolyn Jacob, Stephen Done and Simon Eckley, 1994
Copyright © photographs Merthyr Tydfil Borough Council and
contributors,1994
Alan Sutton Limited
12 Riverside Court
Bath BA2 3DZ

ISBN 0 7524 0012 6

Typesetting & origination by
Alan Sutton Limited
Printed in Great Britain

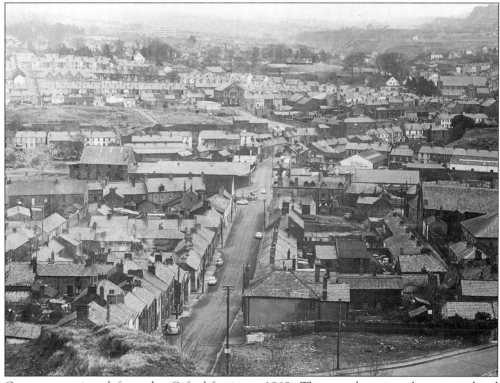

Georgetown viewed from the Cyfarthfa tips, c.1969. The area has since been completed redeveloped.

Contents

First World War memorial at Pontmorlais designed by L.S. Merrifield. The three sculpted figures which represent St Tydfil, a miner and a mother with child later attracted the praise of Poet Laureate Sir John Betjeman.

Public Offices, Merthyr Tydfil, 1904.

Introduction

By Her Worship the Mayor, Councillor Mrs L.A. Matthews.

I was very pleased to see the draft of this publication, and to glimpse again the unique history of a proud Borough. The Merthyr Valley is too rich in both industrial and social history to make a definitive photographic record possible, but I believe that this selection reflects many key aspects of the area as it was, and as it is remembered.

Although these photographs come from the collections at the Library and Museum, in a very real sense they all belong to the people of Merthyr Tydfil. As a Borough we boast that our superb collections of photographs have been built up through the generosity of hundreds of local people. I understand that in the week that followed the first draft of the book no fewer than 37 new photographs were brought to the library - five of which were added to this book! This public support and involvement is exactly as it should be, because we serve and reflect a living community.

Cyfarthfa Castle Museum and Merthyr Tydfil Public Libraries are both products of the spirit that drove the developments in local goverment when Merthyr Tydfil was granted Borough status in 1905 and County Borough status in 1908. The Museum, occupying, along with the school, the former home of the Crawshay ironmasters, was a symbol of a thriving town whose main industries were coal and steel and which until after the 1914-18 War continued to flourish and grow. While in the dark days of the depression and collapse of the coal industry that followed, the new Carnegie Library became a symbol of hope for the future.

It is sad that the hardships of the 1920's and 1930's have tended to cloud this vibrant social

Lower High Street, 1905.

and economic history and the times when in many senses the town stood at the very centre of national life. Yet Merthyr Tydfil has never lost its role at the centre of the region. Recent improvements to roads, shops, recreational facilities, services and businesses are part of an ongoing regeneration of the Borough. Our people share a heritage and a vision.

We now stand again at an historic point in the development of our community and anticipate the time when we believe that changes in local goverment will allow Merthyr Tydfil to regain control of its future. As we build that future together, we can recall past achievements

Linda A Matthews

Mayor of Merthyr Tydfil

One
Rural Roots

Anni Groves at Penydarren Farm, 1914. A number of important farms were to survive alongside the massive industrial development which took place in the area.

Outside Troedyrhiw Farm, 1900. Mr T. Williams the farmer poses with his champion shire horse. The old name for Troedyrhiw Farm (now the site of Afon Taf High School) was Tir Rhoel Gymrwg and it had been part of the estate of Ifor Bach, Welsh lord of Senghenydd. The last farmer there was Mr William Nathaniel Jones, affectionately known to the people of Troedyrhiw as 'Bill the Farm'.

Farmworkers in the Aberfan area, *c.*1910 with the tools of haymaking.

Before the advent of large scale mechanisation haymaking and other agricultural activities involved the whole family in intensive manual labour. This scene dating from *c.*1914 illustrates the rural origins of many communities within the borough.

Caeracca Farm, Pant, 1896. On the ground is a model of a Dowlais Works locomotive.

High Street, Pontsticill Village in 1904.

Two
Iron and Steel Capital

Cyfarthfa Steel Works, 1904. Molten steel is being cast into ingot moulds using the Bessemer process.

An early photograph (c.1877) of the Cyfarthfa site attributed to Robert Crawshay then master of the ironworks and also a skilled photographer. It is unusual in that there is no discernible activity; the rolling mills and forges having been shut down due to a wages dispute between workers and management (see p. 42).

The Cyfarthfa Steelworks enveloped in smoke, 1894, with the Swansea Road in the foreground. In 1884 the Crawshay brothers had reopened the Cyfarthfa site as a steelworks. However, they were unable to remake the company into a viable concern and in 1902 their shares were acquired by G.K.N. Co. Ltd. of Dowlais. In 1919 the works were finally closed never to open again.

Cyfarthfa Steelworks, c.1900 showing a Peckett locomotive and wagon crossing the rail bridge over the Taff. In the background the blast furnaces can be glimpsed.

Blacksmiths at Cyfarthfa, 1904.

The locomotive 'Cyfarthfa No 4' transporting ladles full of molten iron to the Bessemer converters. One of several inaccurate explanations for the nature of the three sided Pandy Farm clock visible in the background is that it was so built to prevent the workers from knowing the right time.

Limestone workers, 1890's cutting stone to fuel the furnaces at Dowlais. Limestone, plentiful in the Merthyr area, was an essential part of the iron industry. After being brought from the quarries the stone was broken up by girls for use in the smelting.

Ruins of Plymouth Ironworks blast furnace with the chimney of South Duffryn Colliery behind. Derelict from the 1860's the Plymouth works, together with Cyfarthfa, Dowlais and Penydarren, had earlier in the century been part of the quartet of ironworks which dominated Merthyr.

Dowlais Iron Co. furnaces, 1895. From left to right No 11, No 1 and No 3. While in this year a new Bessemer steel plant was constructed alongside the Goat Mill as part of the continual process of modernisation, the Dowlais Iron Company (from 1902 Guest, Keen and Nettlefolds Co. Ltd) had also opened production at another new steelworks and plate mill down at Cardiff. When this Cardiff plant produced steel at greatly reduced costs and with improvements in efficiency faint writing began to appear on the Dowlais wall.

Though Dowlais was still prosperous in 1913 and benefited greatly from the subsequent war-fuelled boom its many inherent, built-in weaknesses were already starkly apparent, namely: overdependence on specialised exports, an isolated 'hill' location and consequent expense on iron ore haulage, concentration on low added value 'heavy' steel production.

Though Dowlais fought bravely to survive, the world-wide depression of 1929-30 finally sealed its fate as a major works. In 1845 Dowlais had been the greatest ironworks in the world and though it never really came to terms with steel production in a sustainable manner its impact on the development of Merthyr in the the nineteenth and early twentieth centuries proved immense.

Dowlais Iron Company Building Department, 1894. These men would have been responsible for the construction of houses for company workers.

Dowlais Works, 1905. Site preparation for a engine house part of the new blast furnace plant. Dowlais House, built in 1818 for Josiah John Guest managing partner of the works, can be seen in the top centre of the picture.

Locomotive No 8 rebuilt at the Dowlais Ivor Works, 1945. The works had a special engineering department which enabled it to construct its own locomotives.

Brickyard girls at the Dowlais Works, 1912. After 1870 mechanisation greatly changed the nature of work in the brickyards. Previous conditions, however had prompted newspaper reports to suggest that 'a more humiliating and ungenial occupation is hardly to be found.' The girls temper the clay with their bare feet 'moving rapidly about, with the clay and water reaching up to the calf. This operation completed , they grasp a lump of clay weighing about 35 lbs., and supporting it upon their bosoms carry it to the moulding table.'

Foundry casting bay at the Dowlais Ifor Works, 1924.

Dowlais with the works behind, 1974. Metal production which began on the site in 1759 finally ceased in 1987.

Bradney Row & Tips, Penydarren 2536

Actually Bradley Row, 1921 and not strictly speaking in Penydarren. The famous 'white tip of Dowlais' is in the background. Don't believe half of what you read on postcards is the lesson to be drawn.

Three

King Coal

Fochriw colliery owned by the Dowlais Iron Company, 1880's. Although not within the Borough the pit and the village of Fochriw which grew around it both owed their existence to Dowlais' prodigious appetite for coal. Pit Row, demolished in the late 1940's is in the foreground.

Mr Williams hauling coal from the Castle Pit, Troedyrhiw, 1897. Sunk in 1869 by the Cyfarthfa Iron Company at its height as a leading exporter of Welsh steam coal it employed 3,381 men. By the year of closure in 1935, however, the number had dwindled to three hundred.

Perthigleision Terrace, Aberfan, 1905. Five proud young miners after their first day of work at the Merthyr Vale Colliery.

Castle Pit, Troedyrhiw, 1913 with Ash Road in the foreground.

The Fountain pictured here in 1907 was dedicated by W.T. Lewis (Lord Merthyr) to the memory of his wife's grandparents Robert and Lucy Thomas, pioneers of the South Wales steam coal trade. Iron mugs on chains were originally present for the use of the thirsty passer-by.

Nixon's Navigation Colliery, Merthyr Vale, 1890's. Founded by the mining pioneer John Nixon the first coal was brought up in 1875 after which Nixon reputedly treated his men to all the beer they could drink. The pit was soon hailed as 'the premier colliery in South Wales' with 2000 miners employed.

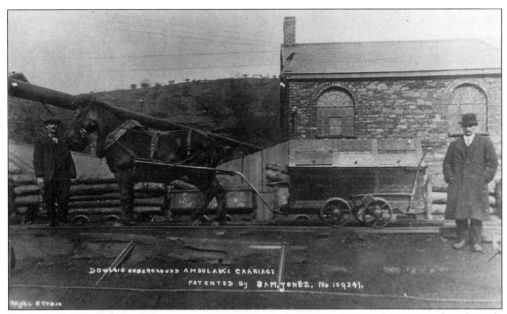

Underground ambulance belonging to G.K.N. Co. Ltd, 1916. An injured man was placed inside the car with the steel doors protecting him from falling debris.

Merthyr Vale and colliery looking east from Aberfan, 1920 s.

A 1912 view of the mining town of Aberfan which was built up around the Merthyr Vale pit. In 1989, this raison d'etre would be ripped out with the closure of the colliery though community spirit still survives.

Aberfan tips and Pantglas school before the disaster, 1960.

Surface workers at South Duffryn Colliery, 1910.

Derelict winding houses from South Duffryn pits, Plymouth Colliery site, 1972.

Dowlais Iron Company's pit at Bedlinog, 1890's. Bedlinog No 1 pit started raising coal in 1881 and Bedlinog No 2 a couple of years later. In 1924 however the colliery was forced to close down and it was not until the opening of the Taff Merthyr colliery at Trelewis later in the 1920's that a major source of employment returned for local men in the Bedlinog area.

Hauliers at Treharris colliery, c.1910. Originally known as 'Harris Navigation' the pit was the deepest in the South Wales coalfield with a distance of 2,280 feet to pit bottom. After a spell as 'Ocean Colliery' its name was changed to Deep Navigation on nationalisation in 1947.

The painful dismantlement process at Deep Navigation Colliery, Treharris in 1991. Closed with the loss of 766 jobs the pit left the nearby Taff Merthyr as the last surviving deep mine in Merthyr borough. Fifteen months later, however, Taff Merthyr too had gone.

Deep Navigation colliery on the day before closure, April 1991. A general view of the entrance with Treharris Boys Club on the left.

This picture from the 1950's shows the site of the Cwmdu drift mine, Heolgerrig. Closed in the 1930's this had been a small operation supplying solely the Cyfarthfa works.

Portrait of a miner at Deep Navigation colliery, 1990 taken by a local photographer

Four
Industrial
Transformation

The old and the new, off Swansea Road, 1950's. Remnants of the Cyfarthfa works closed in 1919, a Hoover depot and top left the Lines Bros factory. The Cyfarthfa site has since been redeveloped further with modern industrial units now housing sucessful businesses such as Morris Cohen.

The button factory (Welsh Products) in 1938 shortly before starting production. The Dowlais Steelworks whose chimneys and silent blast furnaces loom in the distance had employed 4,000 men up to 1930. The new button factory was to employ a mere hundred.

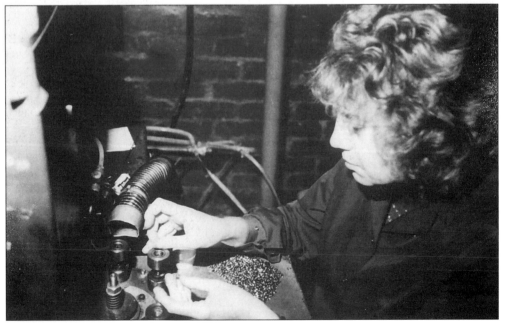

Working in the 'old button factory', 1989

Key war-time industries were relocated to Merthyr Tydfil, an area relatively safe from air attack with, through the ravages of the Depression, abundant local manpower. The Dowlais ICI plant opened in 1938 and made a huge contribution to the war effort through the production of the ammonia needed for explosives. The factory continued long after the war but was finally closed in 1963.

OP Chocolate factory, Dowlais. The original firm of Oscar Pischinger manufactured chocolate and wafer biscuit specialities in Vienna but moved to Wales after Nazi confiscations. Today a French company runs the enterprise.

An aerial view of the Hoover complex, late 1950's. This area had been the site of the Plymouth Ironworks. The Triangle, Pentrebach, a unique example of early Victorian industrial housing is clearly visible in the centre of the picture. It was demolished in December 1977 and the area is now part the Merthyr Tydfil Industrial Park.

Hoover factory floor and workforce, at the opening in 1948 when a total of 350 people were employed. The success of the venture was clearly illustrated 25 years later when the workforce numbered 5,000.

This fleet of Hoover vans illustrates well both that company's progress at Merthyr and the post-war regeneration of the Borough into a centre of light industry.

Men and women at work on the presses, Hoover factory, 1950's. The Hoover factory provided women workers with good wages and financial independence.

Triang factory assembly line, Pentrebach, 1963. In its hey-day Triang was a household name all over the world in the toy industry.

Five
Special Events

An improvised carriage built to celebrate the Coronation of George V, 1911, Pontmorlais promenade, Merthyr.

In 1877 an assembly of workmen from the Cyfarthfa Ironworks gathered to greet Robert Thompson Crawshay on his return from an operation in London to save his sight. They hoped to induce him to re-open the ironworks but were to be disappointed. Crawshay thanked them for their concern but remained implacable on the issue stating that Cyfarthfa would never again become a scene of activity in his lifetime.

The wedding party of Henrietta Louise Crawshay and Captain William Crawshay Ralston on the the steps of Cyfarthfa Castle, 28 April 1871.

In contrast to the Cyfarthfa scene this wedding party (c.1910) is forced to squeeze into the backyard for the post-ceremony shots. Their fine dress, however is an indication of the prosperity of the Borough in the nineteenth and early twentieth centuries.

Town Hall, 1910. The Mayor, surrounded by civil dignitaries, reads the proclaimation address which announced the accession to the throne of George V.

Entrance to the Dowlais Works, 1912. The arch was built of Dowlais coal and erected by craftsmen from the works to celebrate the visit of King George V and Queen Mary.

Red carpet awaiting the footsteps of King George and Queen Mary, 27 June 1912. On the left-hand side is Dowlais House and in the centre 'A' blast furnace and blowing house. The celebrations have been well described as 'a magnificent exhibition of a still great works.'

The Royal Couple, Dowlais, 1912.

The 'Goat Mill' steel arch also constructed in honour of the 1912 royal visit. Having entered through the coal arch (see p. 45) the Royal couple, their tour of the works completed, emerged onto Dowlais High Street through this gate.

A demonstration against the imprisonment of alleged rioters on the road above Taff Merthyr Colliery, 1936. 'Company unionism' caused major disturbances and labour troubles in which 52 men and women received prison sentences. Mr Justice Humphreys outraged Welsh opinion by describing Bedlinog as a 'disgrace to the valleys' and one Margaret Jenkins as 'that wild woman' for pulling a man from his bicycle. These disturbances in Bedlinog revealed a new spirit of revolt and a great determination to fight for economic existence.

Parade in High Street, 1890's.

Prince George (later George VI) in Sand Street, Dowlais, December 1931. He visited the social and educational club for unemployed workers in Horse Street, conducted by the Quaker, John Dennithorne. Sand Street was demolished in 1935.

Would you give this man a job as a brickie? Edward VIII at the Pentrebach training centre, November 1936 picking up skills in cement mixing and sharing a joke with a group which included Sir Kingsley Wood, Minister of Health (left) and Mr Ernest Brown, Minister of Labour (behind).

Tremendous damage was wreaked at Edwardsville, Treharris on Monday 27 October 1913 when the 'Taff Vale Tornado' struck. One report talked of men 'lifted from their feet and dashed to the ground'.

VE Day 1945, St.Mary Street, Twynrodyn.

VE street party, Treharris, 1945.

One of the four parties that took place in Picton Street, Caedraw on VE Day. Due to the barrels of beer that were being emptied at each one a policeman (far left) was obliged to monitor proceedings.

VE Day celebrations Cromwell Street, 1945.

Outside the Glove and Shears public house, Court Street on VE Day.

Festival of Britain celebrations, Dowlais, May 1951. With the opening of the Festival on the South Bank of the Thames hundreds of bonfires were lit all over the country to symbolically unite the British people. Numerous events were held throughout Merthyr borough during the week.

Festival of Britain, Cefn Coed, 1951.

Treharris street festooned to celebrate the Coronation of Elizabeth II in 1953. Events within the borough included an impressive pageant presenting a review of British history.

Six

Hanging Around

The scramble to watch visitors at Deep Navigation, Treharris, c.1909.

Parade passing through Pontmorlais Circus in the 1890's on the way to the drill hall. The Owen Glendower pub was on the right.

Church Street, Troedyrhiw, 1905 with the photographer capturing the full attention of everybody.

Family group, 1913.

High Street, Dowlais, 1910, then a flourishing industrial community.

The building of the Public offices, Merthyr Tydfil in 1894, (see p. 7). The craftsmen and apprentices are grouped according to their individual skills - the foremen wear bowler hats. Shortly after the building was completed George Bernard Shaw decribed the Town Hall as a 'terracotta monstrosity'. With its Dutch gables and bay windows it is a perfect example of Victorian municipal architecture.

John Street taken from the railway station, 1880's. The Merthyr Times newspaper closed in 1899. Over the years Merthyr has had a Guardian, Telegraph and Times as well as the Express. The Liberal Club was to the left of the newspaper offices.

Pontyrhun Bridge, Troedyrhiw, c.1925. Troedyrhiw emerged as an important South Wales coal-mining community during the second half of the nineteenth century. Bridge Street was one of the oldest streets in this community.

Merthyr Central railway station in John Street. Many companies shared the G.W.R station including the Brecon and Merthyr and Taff Vale.

Note the tramlines running up the centre of High Street in 1910.

'Under the Arch', Riverside in the 1940's. The picture was taken from a position just inside the old arch with O'Keefe's lodging house on the right. The street ran parallel to the river Taff.

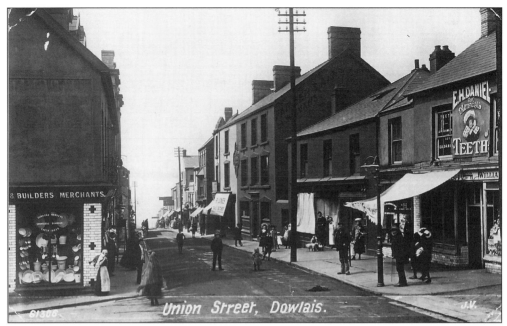

Union Street, 1910. This was the busiest street in Dowlais until its demolition.

Outside 'the Huts' in Treharris in the 1930's. For over a hundred years Treharris remained a close-knit coal-mining community. The wooden accomodation for miners and their families shown here survived to the 1950's.

Seven

Getting Around

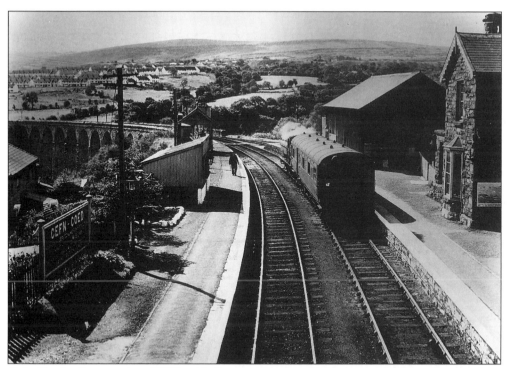

Cefn Coed railway station, 1950's with Swansea Road in the background. The influence of the Crawshay family dictated that the route of the Brecon and Merthyr Railway avoided Cyfarthfa Castle. The Cefn Viaduct, Pontycapel (left) was a considerable engineering feat consisting of fifteen arches.

This picture taken in 1947 shows the path followed by Trevithick's engine along the Penydarren tramroad in 1804.

The Glamorganshire Canal, 1905 with Abermorlais school in the right-hand corner. The open area on the left is now the site of the technical college.

Merthyr's iron bridge, 1963 shortly before it was dismantled and removed to Cyfarthfa Park. Designed by Watkin George it proudly spanned the river Taff in front of Capel Ynysgau.

New Bridge over the river Taff at Cefn Coed on the old border between Glamorgan and Breconshire. Completed in 1910 it was the first ferro-concrete structure in the area.

Pentrebach railway station, 1890's.

This motorised tricycle from about 1905 belonged to the Webley family of Merthyr Tydfil and has an early Glamorgan number-plate.

G.W.R waggon, Treharris, *c.*1912. The railway played a vital part in the delivery of goods in this period the rail network then dominating communications in the valleys.

The Webley family on a motorised tricycle built for two, 1905.

Pontmorlais Promenade, 1914. this photograph and the one below show the re-laying of tramlines in 1914 when large sections of the light railway were renewed and the tramway paved with wooden blocks.

High Street, Merthyr, 1914.

A 1920's Davies bus from Garth Garage, Dowlais stranded in Perrott Pitch, Treharris. The wheel is being changed after an accident.

The main depot of the Merthyr Tramways (the Electric Traction and Lighting Company) was on the site of the old Penydarren Works with the company offices at Pontmorlais. The service was launched in 1901 and operated until 1939 carrying over 85 million passengers and running more than 8 million miles.

Pontmorlais, 1914 part of the series of photographs illustrating the laying of new tramlines.

Agnes Davies, an employee of the Merthyr Electric Traction and Lighting Company, working as a tram conductress in 1917 during the First World War.

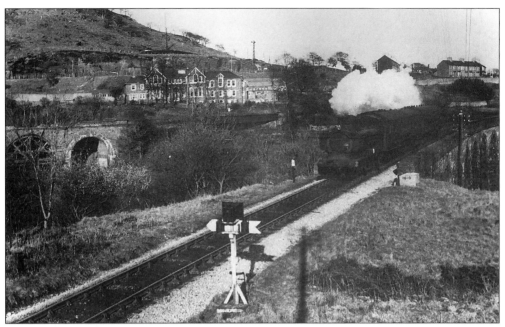

Quaker's Yard Viaduct with the Truant School in the centre.

Taff Vale Station, 1956.

The east platform of Pantyscallog halt, 1913. On the branch line of the London and North West (L.N.W.) Railway which then ran from Abergavenny to Merthyr the halt boasted a station master and porter. The little boy in the dress is Frank Williams.

Merthyr Central station, 1940's. In 1953, after a life of 98 years the overarching roof designed by Brunel began to be removed in stages.

The Gough brothers, Ken, Handel and Percy were early pioneers of bus services in the 1930's. Operating from Cefn Coed, they ran day trips into the Beacons and also to the coast. Further down the valley the small 'Rose Marie' fleet of buses ran from Troedyrhiw and Jones Brothers from Treharris. The Gough buses were sold during the Second World War and D.J.Davies then ran the service to Cefn Coed.

Promotional picture taken outside Cyfarthfa Castle, 1948 for C. Davies and Sons, Garth House, Dowlais. The firm concentrated on coal delivery and removal contracting as well as general haulage, their advertisements promising 'careful removals, distance no object.'

A bus on Glebeland Street, 1964 and in the background the once popular and now sadly demolished Lamb Inn on Castle Street.

A charabanc trip run by Ernie Snow to Combe Martin in 1916. Ernie (seen here reclining on the running-board) was one of the more interesting people in the South Wales motor trade; a self-made businessman he also moonlighted as a boxing promoter and inventor. Although his bus and charabanc service finished in 1936, the Snow garage is still a well-known business in the Merthyr Valley. The pictured coach was called Secundus and on-board entertainment included an organ.

Eight
Leisure

A day trip to the Beacons run by Gough Brothers of Cefn Coed in the 1930's (see p. 74). The cost was one shilling with a stop off for a picnic lunch.

Robert Thompson Crawshay in his 'box', a travelling photographic studio.

Rose Harriette, elder daughter of Robert Thompson Crawshay and a favoured subject for her father's photograhic portraits.

Rose Mary Crawshay on harp accompanied by Mr and Mrs Sutherland on cello and piano, late 1850's. The picture was taken by Roger Williams, then personal secretary to Robert Thompson Crawshay and later a professional photographer in Cefn Coed.

One of the former Crawshay family drawing-rooms in use here in the 1930's as part of the museum and art gallery.

A wagonette of day trippers eager for the off outside St. Mary's Church, *c.*1905. On such outings a cask of ale secured under the driver's seat would have been indispensable in order to 'lay the dust.'

Gellideg Dramatic Society, 1910. Many of the dramatic societies in the borough were associated with individual churches, factories or schools.

Crawshays and friends at their fishing cottage, Scethrog near Llangorse Lake.

Miners on an outing posing in front of an iced-up Ffrwd. The men were all related in some way. Back row left to right: Bert Hunt, Ben Thomas, ? Rogers, Will Thomas. Front row left to right: Fred Trott, James Thomas, Tom Davies. James Thomas lived in the Viaduct Cottages on Pontycapel Rd. and worked underground at Cwm Pit.

The Turkish Baths in Lower High Street owned by the aptly named Mr W. Pool. According to contemporary reports these had a 'conspicuous Eastern aspect' with a hot room which registered 200 degrees of heat (Fahrenheit one hopes) and a shampooing room where 'by scientific manipulation at the hands of a well trained masseur, every nerve and muscle of the human frame is restored to its natural action and elasticity.' Above the bath was 'the acquatic trapeze and swinging apparatus, by means of which the swimmer may launch himself with ease into shallow or deeper water.' Prices ranged from one to two shillings depending on requirements.

Ynysgau, *c*.1885. The arch alongside 'The Parrot' led to Castle Street.

Edwardian public house interior, Temple Bar, High Street Merthyr, 1905.

Exterior of the Temple Bar in 1905 showing the landlord, Mr Evans and his family. This establishment was situated in Lower High Street (near present-day Woolworths) until the 1930's.

Rainbow Inn, Castle Street, 1903. Public houses and the unlicensed 'beer shops' often kept by women were extremely numerous in the Merthyr of those days.

Bike and Atkins family, Dowlais, 1913.

St.Davids dramatic society, Troedyrhiw, 1918 - a celebration of the end of the First World War. The village has always maintained a lively community spirit supporting various clubs and societies.

Cyfarthfa Workmen's Band, 1905. The band was formed by Robert Thompson Crawshay who designed the special uniform and engaged a London conductor for their performances.

Treharris Ladies Jazz band, 1930's.

Picture Palace, Troedyrhiw about 1929. A once popular cinema the building was demolished in 1993.

The Castle Cinema Sunday screening campaign, 1956, part of a national struggle.

Thomastown Park, *c.*1900 with the chimneys of Cyfarthfa Steelworks in the distance.

Porthcawl, 1960's then a popular destination for Wales' and Merthyr's discerning sun-worshippers.

Nine

Trade

Troedyrhiw Co-op, 1912. At the time the President of the Troedyrhiw and District Co-operative Society was Councillor Enoch Morrell, miners leader and first mayor of Merthyr Tydfil. The building is now occupied by Al's Tackle Shop, a butcher's, greengrocer's and a Chinese take-away thereby giving some indication of the scale of the Co-op.

A late 1920's mobile shop and delivery van which operated in the lower part of the valley, especially in the Troedyrhiw area.

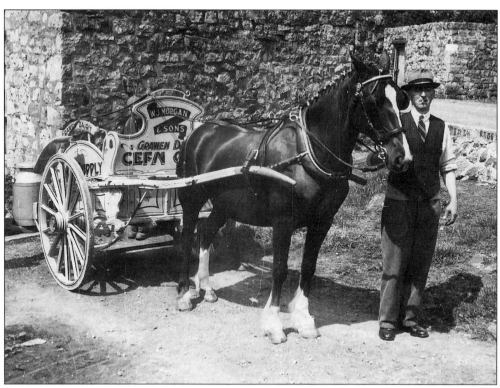

William Morgan's Grawen Diary cart from Cefn Coed pulled by Robin a popular and prize winning animal, 1940's.

C.F. Vining, tobacconist and confectioner, Aberfan, 1940's.

High Street, Caeharris, 1905. While the Dowlais Works were in full operation this was a prosperous commercial area. Caeharris Post Office later featured in a 1930's painting by Cedric Morris now hanging in Cyfarthfa Museum.

Operating in the centre of town, this laundry firm boasted 'shirts and collars our speciality', *c*.1911. Other large laundries operated in the Borough including the Dowlais Sanitary Laundry Co. Ltd, Pant.

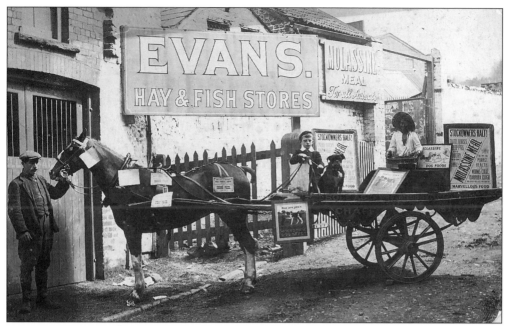

Masonic Street, Merthyr, 1912. This cart, normally used for commercial deliveries, has just won a prize in a parade.

A second decorated cart, Masonic Street, 1912.

Treharris Industrial Co-operative, 1930's.

High Street, Merthyr, 1930's. The
Palace Cafe was noted for providing
food for wedding receptions.

Vehicles belonging to Ferguson Fruit wholesalers outside the Great Western Railway depot, c.1940. The freight handling facilities of each railway station were of vital importance for the growth of trade.

T.D. Rees the Chemist's, Aberfan, 1940's.

Crosswoods, Aberfan in the late 1940's. This general store delivered groceries throughout the Borough.

Interior of Crosswoods also in the late 1940's. Note how many staff this thriving business employed.

Ten

Sport

Pant Cad Ifor pub quoits team c.1900.

Merthyr Intermediate County School hockey team, 1911. Back row, left to right: Mary Collins, Thurston Ellis, Bessy Phillips, Bessy Williams. Middle row: Hilary Lloyd, Gwladys Kenshole, Gwen Francis, Daisy Roberts, Ethel Walters. Front row: Gwladys Francis and Ethel Davies.

Cyfarthfa Juniors RFC, 1906. The industrial remains behind the team were part of Ynysfach Iron Works.

Merthyr Thursdays AFC, 1912/13 season. Their record for the year was most impressive: Played 34. Won 30. Drawn 1. Goals for, 116; against 16. First row: J.Jenkins, E.Edwards, D. Sallis, S.O. Williams, D.T. Evans, P. James. Second row: T.Deen (Hon. Sec.), R.Griffiths, B. Harding, J. Morgans, A.Anderton, E. Jones, G. MacNaught, D.O. Williams, T.H. Williams, H. Prosser. Bottom row: T. James, W.H. Hancock, A.E. Harpur.

Presentation to Arthur Lewis winner of South Wales News Challenge Cup, Gwaunfawr swimming baths, 1925. The previous year the baths had been officially presented by Sir Seymour Berry (Lord Buckland) to the Merthyr Tydfil Corporation and opened to the public on 3 July 1924.

The open air swimming baths at Edwardsville shortly after being opened by the Commissioner for Wales, Captain Crawshay on 27 May 1937. A similar baths opened in Pant the following month.

G.K.N. Co Ltd Welfare football team, 1920-21 season.

Merthyr and District cricket team, 1930's.

Merthyr Intermediate (County) School rugby first XV, 1934. Back row (left to right) Jack Burke, Henry Lewis, Gwyn Williams, John Lewis, ? Jones, Eddie Rowlands, Del Davies, Ossie Bow. Middle row (left to right), Bert Gleneross, Cliff Hopkins, R H Pugh, Bryn Jones, Monty Warrington, Jack Hughes, Leo Davies. Front row (left to right) Jack Price, Eric Evans, E. Williams.

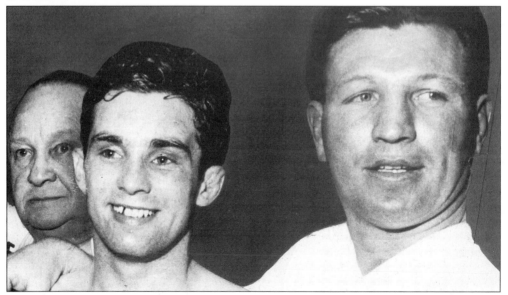

A proud Eddie Thomas with Howard Winstone after winning the British Featherweight title against Terry Spinks, May 1961. Under Eddie's management Winstone went on to claim the world crown later in the decade.

Eleven
Education

Science class at Cyfarthfa, 1914 a year after the opening of the school.

Nursery class, 1898 at the Dowlais School built in 1855 by Lady Charlotte Guest as a memorial to her husband, Sir John Guest.

Girls dawdling to hockey practice at Cyfarthfa Castle Secondary school for girls, 1930's. Pleated tunics, long stockings and ties were regulation wear for games in this period.

Quaker's Yard Truant School, 1905. This institution had been founded in 1896 'to teach the truant boys of the district that they cannot be allowed to persist in their truancy.' Boys rose at 6 a.m. each day to a breakfast of cocoa, bread and dripping and following the evening scripture lesson and prayers, they went to bed at 8 p.m. Corporal punishment was widely used to maintain discipline.

Many of these Treharris schoolboys seen here in 1905 visiting Deep Navigation would have had their working lives dominated by this important colliery.

Treharris Boys School, c 1936. This photograph was possibly taken at summer camp as the boys are standing in an unusually informal manner for the period.

Heolgerrig Infants School, 1930's.

A 1950's Christmas party at Gellifaelog School, Penydarren. In 1972 it became a Welsh medium school.

Gellideg School, shortly after the official opening on 15 July, 1959.

Twelve

Worship

Ruins of Cwm Glo chapel, c.1878. The Merthyr area was a haven of religious dissent with stubborn adherance to belief in the face of official persecution. In 1620 covert worship began at the remote farmhouse of Blaencanaid to the west of Merthyr. Growing congregations soon forced a move to a new meeting place in the thickly wooded valley of Cwmglo. Here a barn was filled with hay in order to allay suspicions only being emptied in time for the Sunday service. Watchmen were posted to warn of approaching danger. After the 1689 Toleration Act permitted public worship the Dissenters were able to build the chapel at Cwm Glo. However in the second half of the eighteenth century this fell into disuse when the new Ynysgau chapel was opened in the centre of Merthyr. Photo: R.T. Crawshay.

The Ynysgau dramatic society poses inside the chapel, 1906. The Ynysgau Independent Welsh Chapel had a large congregation, which included the family of the Dowlais ironmaster, John Guest.

Iron bridge leading to the Ynysgau chapel, c.1953. Built in 1749 and remodelled in 1853 it was a fine example of late classic chapel architecture. It was demolished in the 1960's.

View from the tip in Georgetown looking down on Chapel Row, birthplace of the composer Joseph Parry, together with the complete chapel, 1910. The Dowlais works are visible in the far distance.

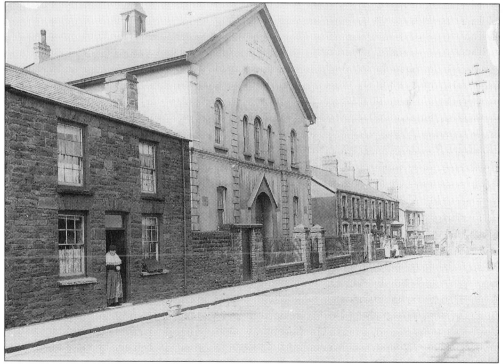

Y Deml Baptist Church, Abercanaid, 1904. Founded in 1835 the building has now been demolished.

Dowlais Temperance Choir competition winners at Crystal Palace, July 1895 where they were winners of the first prize in the premier competition for choirs. The conductor was A.J.Rees. The musical tradition in the Borough is outstanding and flourished even in the dark days of the depression. In the late 1930's at a time when nearly 80% of male choir members were unemployed, both the Dowlais and Merthyr Tydfil United Choir and the Merthyr Philharmonic Choir won the chief choral competition at the National Eisteddfod.

Supporters of the Religious revival of 1904 amidst slag heaps and mining debris, Aberfan. The *Western Mail* reported on 15 December 1904 that people 'gather together in hundreds and sing and pray in the streets at Midnight.....people made the hills resound at Aberfan last night. They had heard Evan Roberts at Merthyr Vale, and had carried his enthusiasm across the river.'

The Dowlais Christian Mission dressed in their Sunday best for a rally in Pontypool, 1910.

The first Ynysowen choir pictured here in 1910 was mostly concerned with religious music. The present-day Ynysowen Male Voice Choir is also noted for its charitable work.

Outside St. Cynon's parish church at Fiddler's Elbow, c.1908.

St John's Church, Dowlais, 1973. The original building was built by Josiah John Guest, but as the town of Dowlais grew so too did the church. It contains many memorials to the leaders of the iron and steel industry; the Nave window showing Christ in Majesty above two miners at a coal face is in memory of the Martin family.

Thirteen
Service to the Community

James Keir Hardie, founder of the modern Labour Party and first Independent Labour MP for Aberdare and Merthyr (1900-15) seen here atttending a social event in Troedyrhiw, 1910.

Cyfarthfa Castle, 17 September 1910. A group of local dignitaries including Mr James the Mayor and Lord Glanusk at the opening of the ground floor as a museum and art gallery. Built in 1825 and occupied by the Crawshay family for sixty-five years, Cyfarthfa Castle was bought by the Merthyr Tydfil Corporation in 1909 for £19,700.

R.C. Wallhead, one of the builders of the Independent Labour Party, 1930. Imprisoned as a conscientious objector during the First World War he was elected M.P. for Merthyr at the election of 1922. At his death in 1934 he was succeeded by S.O. Davies.

Awarding the title of freeman of the Borough of Merthyr Tydfil to the Prime Minister, Clement Atlee, 18 April 1946. In the centre is S.O. Davies MP who represented the borough at Westminster from 1934 to 1972.

A division of the Glamorgan constabulary outside the Central Police Station in Graham Street, Merthyr Tydfil in June 1912. These extra officers were needed to maintain order and clear the streets for the royal visit and address at the Town Hall. The Chief Constable was later congratulated for his good work by the Merthyr Watch Committee. The first Bernie Bros cafe can be seen in the background.

A detachment of Merthyr police under the command of Sgt. Botting outside the Central Police Station in 1912. To enable them to clear the streets ahead of the royal visit they were seated on horses borrowed from local residents.

Merthyr Tydfil Fire Brigade engine, 1932. This particular Leyland model replaced the Morris fire engine which after 21 years of service had been sold to an Abergavenny farmer for £13 5s 0d.

Outside the Vaynor ward, Mardy Central Isolation Hospital shortly after it was opened by Keir Hardie in 1907. The hospital grounds originally contained a sizable garden.

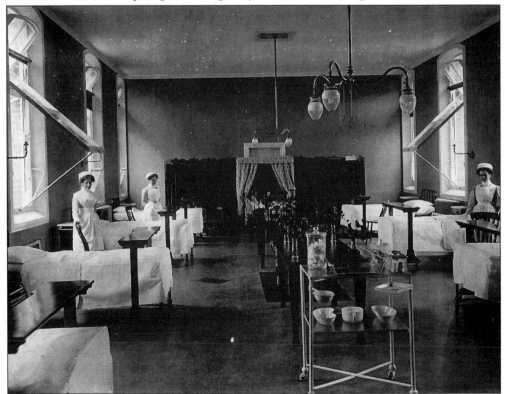

The new Vaynor ward at Mardy Hospital, 1907. During its first year 150 patients were admitted, mainly cases of scarlet fever, typhoid and diphtheria.

Lance Rogers from Cefn Coed (back right) and other men who joined the International Brigade in 1937 to fight against the fascist forces of Franco in Spain.

Home Guard, 1944. The Civil Defence Organisation was required to keep a complete card index listing each person in the borough. In 1943, Sir John Hodsell, Inspector General of Civil Defence had found 'a magificently keen and good organisation.'

9th (Glamorgan) Battalion of the Home Guard, 1943.

Treharris St John's Ambulance nursing cadet division, 1949, with Dr Robson in the centre. The picture was taken the year Treharris ambulance cadets, student cadets and nursing cadets all won prizes at the Royal National Eisteddfod.

Civic buildings, Portmorlais, 1910. In November 1936 Edward VIII visited the Labour Exchange there. A newspaper report of the time records that the voice of suffering spoke through one unemployed man who cried 'we want work your Majesty'. Shortly afterwards the King who had stated 'something must be done' was himself also out of a job, if not out of pocket, following his abdication.

Acknowledgements

We are very grateful for the support of the following individuals, not least in giving their permission for photographs to be reproduced.

Mr J.A. Owen, Mr Bill 'Engine' Jones (for enthusiastically borrowing material from other people), Dr T.F. Holley, Mr S. Richards, Mr D. Phillips, Mrs E.M. Smith, Mr C. Thomas, Mr L. Davies, Mrs V. Rees, Mr D. Morgan, Mr Beynon, Miss C. Owen, Mr F. Williams, Mr Parry, David Watkins, Dr H. Crann, Mr D.A. Cole, Mrs M. Gough, Mr P. Rogers, Mrs I. Thomas, Miss M. Morgan, Mrs D. Watkins, Mrs Rees, Ms M. Hughes, Mr P. Williams, Mr D. Hamer, Mr Thomas, Mr G. Bowen, Mr Case, Miss Collins, The Davies Family, Mr Morgan, Mr Brian Thomas, Mrs Grey, Mrs Cutriss-Steels, Mr G. Arnold, Mrs N. Jones and Mr. M. Hale. The Welsh Industrial and Maritime Museum and Merthyr Tydfil Historical Society. Councillor Oswald Griffiths, Councillor W.A. Rogers and Councillors E. and K. Thomas.

Mr Ted Rowlands MP.

A special thanks to the staff at the Library, Museum and other Council Departments for their support.

We apologize for any omissions and invite anyone with similar, or better, images of the Borough of Merthyr Tydfil to join the individuals listed above in allowing us to copy your photographs and thereby preserve our heritage.

High Street, Penydarren.